Walking Guide to Windsor and Eton

A suggested walking guide around Win
visitors who would like to take in most
spending any money at all! This is a circuit route which can be
joined at any point on the route.

Start off at the Coach Park, most visitors to Windsor either come
in by Coach or park in the main car park alongside the Alexandra
Gardens. Visitors that arrive via the train station

Avoid the shops and walk into Alexander Gardens via one of the
two entrances to the left of the shops in the Car Park.

1/ spot the large tree in the center and try to identify the
approximate age and type of tree. In warm weather this is a great
place to picnic or listen to bands that perform on the Bandstand.

2/ Turn left along the path and walk towards the crazy golf, and
children's play area. You may want to allow your children to
amuse themselves here and let off steam, especially if they have
travelled a long time getting to Windsor.

3/ Keep walking west towards the railway arches and exit the
Gardens through the Gate. Cross the road towards the river. In
Summer there are model railway rides and popular children's
rides.

Look out for the full-scale Hawker Hurricane World War 2
Aeroplane. Read the write up about a famous Windsor resident
that helped design the engine.

4/ The river here is busy with canoe rentals and cabin cruisers.
The island ahead is Bath Island. Walk towards the river and turn
right

and take the path alongside the river. The swans and geese are
likely to watch you and seek food should you have any?

5/ Continue walking past the Ice Cream Hut and small island. You are likely to pass cabin cruisers and day boat berthed. Motorboats and rowing boats are readily available for hire in the summer months. Further along the path you will see larger boats that take visitors for river trips lasting around an hour. Tickets can be purchased from a wooden hut close by.

6/ stick to the path leading to the Bridge and note the famous St Christopher Wren Hotel on the right, whilst ascending the steps to the Bridge.

7/ Cross over the bridge into Eton. This is a good place to take photographs. Continue across the bridge but turn sharp left at the George Pub into Brocas Street. You will pass the rear of Eton Boys Boat House and smart town homes overlooking the Thames.

8/ Continue to the end of the Street onto a large common grass area called the Brocas. To gain the great views of Windsor Castle walk alongside the river westwards and turn back for the best views of the castle.

9/ Cut back across the Brocas (see map) away from the river to the Meadow Lane car park. Walk into the car park and out the other side through a gate and into another common grass field called The Meadow. The path leads straight towards a building resembling a crown, which is the Eton Museum of Antiquities, part of Eton College. Exit

through the gate in front of the building.

10/ Turn right into South Meadow Lane and follow the road to Keats Lane bearing right and onto Eton High Street. You are likely to pass numerous Eton College boys and staff in their elegant uniforms during term times.

11/ When reaching the junction of Slough Road and Eton High Street turn right into Eton High Street. Tours of Eton Collage can be arranged to the left off Slough Road look for signs. Fees may be required for tours of the college and they are generally guided.

12/ The High Street comprises of numerous shops, many aimed at students at the college for uniforms, and other clothing. There is also an interesting book shop full of very old books, antique shops, and hotels, pubs, wine bars and restaurants.

13/ Make your way back towards the bridge, perhaps stopping for refreshments of a bite to eat. Cote Brasserie to the left of the bridge before crossing the bridge is popular with tourists since it overlooks the river.

14/ Once across the bridge, walk directly ahead into Thames Street, passing the St Christopher Wren Hotel. You will next enter a busy junction on Datchet Road.

15/ Turn left towards Windsor and Eton Riverside Station. The route can be started here for visitors who arrive by train from London. Walk past the station and look out for a building built to accommodate Queen Victoria as she waited for a train to take her to London. This building was designed by the architect Tite.

16/ Home Park lies ahead but unless these playing fields are busy with archery, rugby or horse events, it's best to turn around and head back towards town.

17/ Cross the road by the station using the zebra crossing. At the corner you will see a memorial to King George V designed by the famous architect Edwin Lutyens. Keep left and walk up the slope towards the castle, passing bus stops, and take in a view of Windsor's Theatre Royal.

18/ Continue on keeping the castle on your left, and opposite the busy shop's restaurants and pubs, unless you want to stop and eat?

19/ As you pass the taxi rank, you will approach a statue of Queen Victoria. Turn Left and walk towards the main entrance to the castle. This is the famous Henry XIII gate and is usually flanked by armed police. This is a good picture opportunity. It is possible to pay the entrance fee to the castle around here and queues are generally lengthy in the summer months.

20/ take the street opposite the gate which is Church Street, a quant cobbled street with shops and tee rooms. This was the market area in years gone by with fishmongers and butchers busy displaying food for the Royal kitchens. Look for Nell Gwynn's house, mistress to Charles II.

There were rumours that a secret passage underground linked this area to the castle, so visitors could make their visits in secret!

21/ Take the next right and turn into Queen Charlotte's Street. This is reputed to be the shortest street in England, just 51 feet long!

22/ The building to your immediate left is the famous crooked house. It has been used over the years as a tea room and jewelers' but currently stands empty. Great photo opportunity.

23/ you are now in the High Street and a left turn and a few steps up will take you under the Guild Hall. A museum here is often open and run by knowledgeable volunteers and well worth a visit if open. Look out for the columns designed by the architect, which don't hold up the room above!Public toilets to the front of the Guild Hall are available down some steps below street level. As well as kings and queens who have married here, Elton John also got married here.

24/ Walk past the Guild hall to Church Lane, popular with tourists having numerous restaurants. The pub facing you in Market Street called the Three Tuns has a note about its history to the right of the front door.

25/ Turn back to the High Street and continue away from the castle and pass the Windsor Parish Church of St John the Baptist. Entrance here is welcome and free.

Continue to the next road junction where you will see a statue of a modern soldier and a rare Post Box in blue.

26/ Keep left into Park Street and continue along the road towards the entrance to the Long Walk. Just before entering the through the gates you will notice a quant old pub to your left called the Two Brewers. This pub has a long history and is well worth a stop on a sunny day however it's probably the most popular pub in Windsor, so prepare to wait for a drink!

27/ Enter the park and to your left you will see the entrance to the State Apartments on Windsor Castle. This is where Royalty stay and is generally not open to the public.

Guards usually flank the main entrance to the apartments and can be generally seen from a distance from the closed gates. Good photo opportunity here. Turning around you will take in the view of the famous Long Walk. On a clear day you can see all the way to the Statue of the Copper Horse. Residents and visitors of Windsor frequently

walk this route, but it's lengthy and I have omitted it from this guide as there is still much left to see.

28/ Reverse your route back along the same Park Street and passed the Two Brewers pub. At the end of the road keep right into St Albans Street which borders the castle walls. On the right you will notice another entrance to the castle most frequently used for staff and workers to the castle. There are also stables to house the horses here and carriages frequently used in State occasions. Eventually you will renter Castle Hill again, just turn to your left and walk down towards the Statue of Queen Victoria. Cross the road by the crossing and head down hill into Peascod Street.

29/ Peascod Street has a wealth of eating coffee and other shops. Notably Daniels a fine store for clothes and children's toys on the first floor. Spend time here but when finished head back to a narrow Lane between two shoe shops (Jones And Ecco shoes) this is Goswell Hill.

30/ Walk this narrow cobbled lane to some steps and proceed upwards into the busy Central Station concourse. Lots of shops and restaurants here to look at. Eventually turn towards the main station and away from the castle. Trains here will take you to Slough, and connect with trains from other regions. To return to the Coach Station avoid the platform for the trains and walk to the right of the train platform, along a walkway towards the foot bridge ahead. Lifts and steps will return you to the shops by the coach Station.

Windsor in England is a great place to explore and enjoy. The Theater Royal, a historic theater built in 1883, offers an array of live entertainment from musicals to comedy shows. Visitors should not miss the opportunity to take a guided tour of Windsor Castle, one of the official residences of Her Majesty the Queen and the largest inhabited castle in the world. For those who appreciate nature, a visit to Eton Boat House will be an unforgettable experience. Here visitors can go boating on the lush River Thames and admire the beautiful wildlife that inhabits the riverbanks. With so much to see and do, Windsor is sure to provide a wonderful holiday experience. Whether you're looking for a day of sightseeing or an afternoon of leisure, there's something for everyone in Windsor. So why not take the time to explore all that this wonderful town has to offer? You won't regret it! Theater Royal is one of the most popular attractions in Windsor. Situated in the heart of town, Theater Royal continues to entertain with its unique mix of drama, comedy and music. From classic plays to contemporary performances, Theater Royal has something for everyone. Whether you're a theater enthusiast or just looking for a great night out, Theater Royal should not be missed. So come and experience all that Windsor has to offer – from its stunning architecture to its amazing cultural offerings. There's so much to do and see – make sure you don't miss out!

Windsor is full of things to do; explore it today! You won't regret it. Get ready for an unforgettable experience!

Start by visiting the magnificent Windsor Castle. Built in the 11th century and home to the British royal family, Windsor Castle offers a glimpse into Britain's history and heritage. You can also take a leisurely stroll around the beautiful grounds of Eton Boat House or take a boat ride along The River Thames for breathtaking views of Windsor. Visit Theater Royal for a night of entertainment or explore Windsor Great Park for an outdoor adventure – there are plenty of things to do in Windsor!

So come and explore all that Windsor has to offer – from its stunning architecture to its amazing cultural offerings. There's so much to do and see – make sure you don't miss out! With Theater Royal, Windsor castle, Eton boat house and much more, you're sure to have an unforgettable experience. Enjoy your time in Windsor!

The Windsor Bridge in Windsor, England is another key attraction in the area. The bridge replacement was completed in 1992 and spans the river Thames between two sides of the town of Windsor. The bridge replacement was designed by French engineer Eugène Freyssinet and took nine years to complete. Constructed as an arch-shaped road bridge, the replacement features a main span of 276 meters and a total length of 473 meters. The bridge replacement is composed of steel, reinforced concrete and glazed pottery, making it an impressive feat of engineering.

The Windsor Bridge replacement has become a tourist attraction in its own right for visitors to the area – particularly for those interested in engineering. The replacement also provides an invaluable transport link between the two sides of Windsor, allowing locals to go about their daily lives. As a replacement, it is a fitting tribute to its predecessor and has become an iconic symbol of England's renowned heritage.

It was originally constructed in 1828 by John Rennie and Sons, a prominent British civil engineering firm. [1] The bridge was later renovated in 2002 by the Royal Borough of Windsor and Maidenhead. [1] In 2012, the Windsor-Detroit Bridge Authority (WDBA) was established to oversee the construction of the Gordie Howe International Bridge. [2] The replacement Windsor Bridge is currently in the planning stages and is expected to be built by Bridging North America, the private concessionaire contracted to construct the Gordie Howe Bridge. [2] The new bridge will be constructed over the Hawkesbury River, 35m downstream of the existing bridge. [3]

References:

[1] Windsor Bridge - Wikipedia

[2] Project Profile: Gordie Howe International Bridge

[3] Windsor Bridge Replacement - Verdict Traffic

The Queen Victoria's Train Waiting Room was constructed in 1842, at the behest of Queen Victoria, at London's Paddington Station. The reception room was designed in a unique Tudor style and was intended to be a private space for the Queen and her entourage to wait for their trains. The room was later expanded and enlarged in 1867, and the original ceiling was replaced with a larger vaulted ceiling. The room was also redecorated in a more ornate style, and the walls and ceiling were painted with floral and heraldic motifs. The room was in use until the mid-20th century and is now open to the public as a museum, which features artifacts and photographs related to Queen Victoria's reign.

At the time it was built, the waiting room provided passengers on the London to Windsor line of the Great Western Railway access to Windsor castle without having to cross private land or enter through any of its gates. As such, it became known as 'Queen Victoria's Train Waiting Room'. Inside, Queen Victoria and her family waited for their arrivals and departures in privacy and comfort. It was also used by other important dignitaries and members of the Royal Household.

Today, Queen Victoria's Train Waiting Room is a Grade II listed building and remains a popular tourist destination, offering visitors insight into life in Victorian England. Restored to its original condition, it still retains many of its period features such as interior paneling, stained glass windows, and ornate fireplaces. Outside, the wrought iron gates remain in place and the latticed trelliswork on the roof has been kept intact. The waiting room is open for visits throughout the week and provides an interesting reminder of how transportation once was. It is also a short walk away from Windsor Castle, the official residence of The Queen. Visitors to the Train Waiting Room can take a step back in time and experience how travel was once conducted at the height of the Victorian era.

For many years, Queen Victoria's Train Waiting Room served as an important symbol of her status as monarch and provided a comfortable space for members of the Royal Household to wait before continuing their journey. The waiting room features luxurious furnishings that were designed exclusively for the Queen, and it was affectionately known among courtiers as "the little palace" due to its grand décor. Other than its use by members of the royal family, it was also frequented by many dignitaries and foreign ambassadors, who were taken to Windsor Castle by train.

The Train Waiting Room is adorned with rosewood paneling and showcases a large fireplace, mahogany chairs, and several other pieces of exquisite furniture that were crafted during the reign of Queen Victoria. The room also features original paintings that depict scenes from her life and works of art commissioned for the royal family. Additionally, visitors can also admire some of the precious objects given as presents to Queen Victoria from her foreign counterparts.

It has been said that Queen Victoria herself often used the Train Waiting Room as a hide-away from her duties, where she would take a respite from her hectic schedule and enjoy some peace and quiet. Today, visitors can enjoy this same atmosphere while they explore its unique features and admire the furniture, artworks, and artifacts which offer an intimate look at life during Queen Victoria's reign. It's simply not to be missed!

This one-of-a-kind space serves as an enduring reminder of British heritage and grandeur, giving visitors an inside look at the life of royalty during Victorian times. It is an important piece of history that still holds great significance today. Take a journey back in time and experience Queen Victoria's Waiting Room for yourself!

The blue letter box is an iconic part of the British postal system. These blue boxes have been around since the 19th century, and they're still in use today. The blue letter boxes are present on nearly every street corner in the United Kingdom. The boxes are usually colored blue, though they can vary in size, shape, and color depending on the area. The boxes are used to deposit letters and parcels, and they are emptied regularly by postmen and postwomen. The blue letter boxes are an important part of British culture, and they are often featured in films, television shows, and books. They are a symbol of reliability and a reminder of a time when communication was much slower.

Additionally, visitors to Windsor Castle can also find the iconic blue letter box and Soldier Statue located outside the castle. The blue letter box was originally installed in 1856 by Queen Victoria and has since become a symbol of British Royalty. The Soldier Statue was commissioned by King George V in 1923 to honor those who served in World War I. Both these structures stand as important reminders of Windsor Castle's long history and its importance to the monarchy throughout the centuries.

Visitors who take their time exploring Windsor Castle often find themselves captivated not only by its architecture but also by what it represents: a window into Britain's past through which we can learn about life during the Victorian era. From Queen Victoria's Waiting Room to the iconic blue letter box, Windsor Castle is filled with symbols of British history and culture.

At the other end of Windsor Castle's grounds is a bronze Soldier Statue which stands guard over the castle entrance. This statue was erected in 2003 by the Royal Borough of Windsor and Maidenhead to commemorate fallen soldiers from Windsor who died during World War II. The statue stands 7' tall and is a reminder that Windsor Castle has served as a symbol of hope and resilience throughout its history.

Both the Blue Letter Box and Soldier Statue are important monuments that honor Windsor Castle's past and serve as lasting reminders of Windsor's contribution to Britain's history. They offer visitors an opportunity to reflect on Windsor Castle's rich past, while also recognizing the sacrifice of those who fought for their country.

Those who gave so much during WWI and beyond. The Soldier Statue, which stands guard outside Windsor castle, was also installed in 1921 in honor of those who sacrificed their lives for their country. Its bronze figure symbolizes courage and strength of spirit - a silent tribute to Britain's fallen heroes. Both the blue letter box and the Soldier statue are important reminders of Windsor Castle's long history and service as Britain's home front during two World wars. They serve as solemn reminders of the brave men and women who fought for our freedom then and now.

The Crooked House of Windsor in Windsor, England was built in 1592 on the edge of the town's market square — thus its older name of the Market Cross. [2] It was initially a private home, and it's unclear who the original owners were. However, records indicate that the house was owned by a number of prominent figures throughout its history, including the Duke of Clarence and the Duke of Gloucester. [1] The house was renovated and rebuilt in 1687, and it's still standing today.

References:

[1] Crooked House of Windsor - Wikipedia[2] The Crooked House of Windsor[3] The Crooked House of Windsor • Historic … - Secret London

The Crooked House of Windsor is an 18th-century timber-framed building located in the grounds of Windsor Castle, England. It is known for its unique design and its intriguing history. The house was first built in 1789 as a folly by George III's son Edward, Duke of Kent and Strathearn, who wanted to create a picturesque structure to enjoy from his apartments at the castle nearby. The house has three floors, each sloping downwards at an angle so that it appears crooked from any angle. Although no one knows why it was designed this way originally, some believe it was to provide spectacular views across open countryside or to fit in with the surrounding landscape. Today, the Crooked House serves as a popular tourist attraction, with visitors able to enter the building and explore its history. It is also popular for taking photographs as it provides a unique backdrop for all kinds of occasions. Despite its crooked design, the house is structurally sound and has survived for over two centuries, making it a fascinating piece of architectural heritage. Visitors are welcome to learn more about this peculiar structure at Windsor castle all year round.

Along with its interesting, crooked design, the Crooked House boasts an intriguing history that adds to its charm. The Duke of Kent commissioned Sir Jeffry Wyat Ville to create this folly in 1789, who was also responsible for remodeling Windsor Castle and creating Buckingham Palace. Since then, the house went through various renovations and changes until it was eventually restored to its original design.

The Crooked House of Windsor is a popular tourist attraction located at Windsor castle in England. The house was built sometime in the mid-seventeenth century and has since undergone several renovations and additions, including two chimneys on its roof. The crooked walls of the house were caused by a combination of subsidence due to water damage as well as structural faults. Today, the building has been restored to its original state with added modern features such as electric lights and fireplaces. It is part of a larger group of buildings around Windsor castle that have been deemed historical monuments and protected from further renovations or alterations.

The Statue of Queen Victoria, located at the foot of Castle Hill in Windsor, was commissioned as part of the Queen's Golden Jubilee celebrations in 1887. It was paid for by public subscription and was sculpted by Joseph Edgar Boehm. The statue was unveiled with much pomp and ceremony on 22 June 1887. [1] A canopy was erected over the statue for the Diamond Jubilee in 2002. [2]

References:

[1] Statue of Queen Victoria ! Yale Center for British Art

[2] "Statue of Queen Victoria at the foot of Castle Hill, Windsor," by …

[3] Queen Victoria Statue at Windsor Castle in Windsor, England

The Statue of Queen Victoria stands at the foot of Windsor Castle in Windsor, England. It is a bronze memorial statue of Queen Victoria that was commissioned by her son Edward VII to commemorate his mother's Diamond Jubilee, held in 1897. The statue was made by Sir Thomas Brock and unveiled on Ascension Day 1903. It stands atop an octagonal Portland stone plinth with four steps, located just outside the gates of Windsor Castle. It depicts the queen in coronation robes and regalia holding a scepter in her right hand and an orb in her left. Inscriptions around the base are written both in Latin and English, honoring

Victoria's reign over Britain for 60 years between 1837-1897. The statue has become a popular tourist attraction and offers a unique glimpse into Windsor's royal connections. It is particularly pleasing to see the queen looking out over Windsor Castle, which she loved so much during her lifetime. It serves as a reminder of Windsor's long-standing connection with royalty, and its place in Britain's proud history. It is truly a sight to behold!

The statue of Queen Victoria was sculpted by Sir Alfred Gilbert in 1893 and is an impressive 15ft tall. It depicts the Queen dressed in regal robes with a scepter and orb in her hands, representing her power over the realm. The inscription on the pedestal reads "Victoria Regina" - Latin for "Queen Victoria".

-- == ++

Multiple Choice Questions:

Which statement best describes the purpose of the Statue of Queen Victoria at Windsor Castle?

A. To commemorate Windsor's history with the monarchy

B. To celebrate Windsor's connection with The Queen

C. To show Windsor's commitment to preserving tradition

D. All of the above

Answer: D. All of the Above.

The Hawker Hurricane was a British single-seat fighter plane that was used by the Royal Air Force (RAF) during World War II. It was the first RAF plane to be equipped with an engine-driven supercharger, which allowed it to fly at higher altitudes and faster speeds than other fighters of its era. The Hurricane was instrumental in defeating the Luftwaffe in the Battle of Britain and went on to serve in other theatres of World War II. It was also used extensively in the Mediterranean, North African, and Southeast Asian theatres. The Hurricane was eventually replaced by the Supermarine Spitfire in 1941, but still served until the end of the war.

The Hawker Hurricane was a British single-seat fighter aircraft developed in the 1930s. What was its primary role?

A. Ground Attack

B. Air Superiority

C. Close Air Support

D. Reconnaissance

Answer: B. Air Superiority. The Hawker Hurricane was designed specifically for air superiority and became iconic during the Battle of Britain where it fought alongside the Supermarine Spitfire to defend Britain from German attack in 1940. It had impressive speed, agility, and firepower that allowed it to become one of the most successful fighter aircraft of World War II. It was used in all theatres of operation, from the Battle of Britain to Burma and the Arctic Ocean. It also saw service with other Allied countries such as Canada, South Africa and Australia. The Hawker Hurricane is still revered today for its part in winning the war for Britain and its allies.

The Hawker Hurricane performed a variety of roles including:

A. Ground Attack

B. Air Superiority

C. Close Air Support

D. Reconnaissance

Answer: D. All of the Above. In addition to air superiority, the Hawker Hurricane was capable of ground attack missions, close air support operations, and long-range reconnaissance duties throughout World War II. It proved an incredibly versatile aircraft, making it an invaluable asset to Allied forces. In combat, the Hurricane was credited with destroying more enemy aircraft than any other British fighter, and its pilots quickly distinguished themselves as some of the most capable in the world.

The Hawker Hurricane has since become a symbol of victory and resilience during World War II. Its design paved the way for later generations of fighters, and it stands as one of the most successful aircraft designs in aviation history. Even today, it continues to inspire awe and admiration from historians and aviation enthusiasts alike. The Hawker Hurricane is truly a timeless classic that will always be remembered for its incredible contributions to victory during World War II. This legendary fighter provided the Allies with an invaluable advantage in the skies during a crucial time in human history. It is an iconic representation of courage and perseverance, and its legacy will live on forever.

To commemorate its achievements, many replicas of the Hawker Hurricane have been built to honor its contributions. The Royal Air Force Museum has even dedicated a full-size replica of this aircraft as a tribute to all who flew it during World War II. Through these efforts, future generations can experience the majesty of this amazing warplane for years to come. With its unique combination of strength and maneuverability, the Hawker Hurricane remains one of the most remarkable aircraft designs ever created.

The story of this legendary fighter will never be forgotten, and its legacy will live on forever. It is a symbol of courage, resilience and hope that remains an inspiration to all who have served in the Armed Forces. The Hawker Hurricane has proven time and time again that it can take on any challenge, no matter how daunting, and come out victorious. Its place in history is undeniable, as it continues to remind us of the brave men and women who put their lives on the line for our freedom decades ago.

Today we remember the Hawker Hurricane for what it stands for: strength under pressure, determination against all odds, and unparalleled skill in flight. This remarkable aircraft will be forever remembered as a reminder of those heroic souls who fought so valiantly during World War II. Its legacy continues to inspire generations of pilots and engineers all over the world, and its spirit lives on in the hearts of those who still take to the skies.

So, when you see a Hawker Hurricane fly overhead, remember with pride the valiant history that it represents. Remember those brave individuals who fought for our freedom and paid such a high price. The legacy of the Hawker Hurricane is one of courage and fortitude - something we should all strive for in our own lives. Thank you for keeping this important piece of history alive.

The Bridge to Bath Island, Windsor, England is a pedestrian bridge that spans the River Thames at Windsor. It was originally built in 1822 and connects the island to the town of Windsor on the western bank of the river. The bridge is made of cast iron and is supported by two arches. It is one of the oldest bridges in the area and is a popular tourist attraction. The island itself is a small area of land, surrounded by the river, which is home to a variety of wildlife, including swans, ducks, geese, and other waterfowl. The bridge is well-maintained and provides easy access to the island from Windsor.

The Eton Boat House in Eton, England was originally built in the 18th century and was used by the college for many years. The building was initially used to store and maintain boats for the college rowing team. It has since been used by other businesses and is now home to a cafe and a gift shop. [1] The building has been well-maintained and is a popular tourist attraction. The building also hosts an annual regatta that is attended by many rowing clubs from across the country. [2]

References:[1] The Eton Boathouses 1870s to the present day[2] The Boat House - Commonwealth Walkway Trust[3] Eton Excelsior Rowing Club - Wikipedia

The Brocas Medow in Windsor, England is an area that has great historical significance. Located on the banks of the river Thames, this meadow has been used for centuries by successive generations as a place to picnic and relax. It is also known for its abundance of wildlife, including numerous species of birds, mammals, and insects. The area has been used as a stopping point for travelers and merchants since Roman times, and the nearby Windsor Castle is believed to have been an important trading hub in centuries past. In more recent history, The Brocas Medow has become a popular spot for visitors looking to experience nature or enjoy a quiet moment of relaxation. Travellers will find plenty of things to do here, such as bird watching, fishing and taking in the beautiful scenery. The meadow is also a great spot for picnics and has plenty of space for outdoor activities. With its rich history and vast array of wildlife, The Brocas Medow is a must-visit destination for anyone looking to experience the beauty of Windsor.

Just a few steps away lies another of Windsor's most beloved attractions: Eton College. Founded in 1440, this prestigious institution offers a world-class education to students from all around the world and it is often referred to as one of the best schools in Europe. Stunning architecture surrounds the college grounds with its impressive Gothic Revival quadrangles and college chapels. In the park outside, visitors can find the iconic Bandstand of Alexander Gardens, which has been a feature of this park since 1892. The bandstand is still used for frequent concerts and serves as an idyllic spot to relax and take in the beauty of Windsor.

Whether you're a student, parent or simply a tourist looking for something to do, Eton College and Alexander Gardens offer a truly unique experience. From the stunning parkland views to the rich history of the college itself, it is certain that you won't be short of things to explore. With its iconic bandstand at its heart, this park is a must-visit for all park-goers looking to embrace history, culture and nature.

Take your time to relax and appreciate the park's stunning views, while also learning more about its unique history. You can even take a few moments to listen to music from the park's bandstand - a perfect way to end your visit! Make sure you don't miss out on this incredible park and all that it has to offer - visit Eton College and Alexander Gardens today!

Eton College's parkland is a great place to spend time outdoors. With its lush green lawns, winding pathways, lakes and park benches, it provides endless opportunity for exploration and relaxation. Alexander Gardens also encompasses the iconic Bandstand - built in 1858 - which hosts popular bands and musicians throughout the year. The park's grounds are perfect for picnicking, taking a leisurely stroll or enjoying some of the park's stun-

The park also offers educational programs on plant life, wildlife and Victorian garden design, allowing visitors to gain an appreciation of its natural beauty and breath-take-

Alexander Gardens is a popular destination for visitors of Eton College, one of the UK's most prestigious independent schools. Located just outside Windsor town center, it is here where students can take part in various sports such as cricket, football and rugby. The park's close proximity to the college also makes it an ideal spot for students to enjoy a break from the classroom.

In addition to its recreational activities, there is also a timeless beauty to be found in Alexander Gardens. The park's Bandstand, built in 1875, stands proud in the middle of a picturesque lake and provides an elegant backdrop for outdoor concerts and events. This monument is symbolic of Eton College's long-standing reputation as one of England's most prestigious educational institutions. There is also a dazzling array of flora and fauna to be found in the park, making it a great place for students, staff and visitors alike to appreciate nature at its finest. All in all, Alexander Gardens offers everything one could expect from one of England's most iconic parks and provides the perfect setting for Eton College's prestigious reputation. Whether visitors come to take a leisurely stroll, observe its majestic architecture or watch a performance

At the Bandstand, Alexander Gardens is sure to delight. The park is a great example of how nature and culture can come together in perfect harmony, making Eton College an ideal destination. With its lush green spaces and stunning historic monuments, the park provides the perfect backdrop for a visit to one of England's most iconic schools. A visit to Alexander Gardens and Eton College is sure to leave visitors in awe of the beauty and grandeur that this park has to offer. In addition to its stunning park, Eton College also features a Bandstand which is used for regular performances by students and local musicians. Sitting at the edge of the park, the Bandstand provides an excellent place to relax and enjoy some music while admiring the park's beauty. Whether you are looking for a peaceful park to explore or an impressive school to visit, Eton College and Alexander Gardens offer something for everyone.

Finally, if you happen to take The Long Walk from Windsor Castle to the Windsor Bridge, you will be rewarded with some of England's finest views. From rolling hills and forests to quaint villages, you'll get a glimpse into what makes Windsor so special. Whether it's for a leisurely stroll or an adventure-filled hike, The Long Walk is sure to take your breath away. So, lace up your walking shoes and don't miss out on one of Windsor's greatest attractions!

The Long Walk is an iconic Windsor walk stretching from Windsor Castle to Windsor Bridge. It has a long and storied history, having been used for ceremonial purposes by the Royal Family for centuries. The pathway provides stunning views of Windsor Great Park, Windsor Castle, and other local landmarks. It's also a great way to connect with Windsor's rich and vibrant history. Along the way, you'll find monuments, statues, and other reminders of Windsor's past.

For those looking for a more adventurous experience, The Long Walk is a great choice. With its winding pathways leading through Windsor Great Park, it offers plenty of opportunities to explore nature and wildlife up close. You'll also find plenty of tranquil spots to relax and take in the views. Whether you're looking for a leisurely stroll or something more energetic, The Long Walk is an ideal destination.

No matter what your reasons are for visiting Windsor, The Long Walk should be on your list of must-see attractions. For centuries its pathways have provided Windsor's royalty with a pleasant walk from Windsor Castle to the River Thames. This path is lined with centuries-old trees, creating a stunning scenic backdrop for Windsor's visitors and offering plenty of striking photo opportunities.

The Long Walk is an iconic Windsor landmark, so don't miss out on the chance to explore it while in Windsor! It features a number of carefully designed viewpoints, benches, and statues that make it the perfect spot for an afternoon stroll or a leisurely picnic.

The Long Walk has been a part of Windsor for centuries, serving as a popular walking route, as well as a popular venue for royal occasions. In more recent times, the Long Walk has been the setting of a number of historic landmarks and activities, including Windsor Castle's Changing of the Guard ceremony and Windsor Horse Show.

Whether you are looking for a peaceful walk in Windsor or simply want to explore Windsor's beautiful scenery and historic landmarks, The Long Walk is a must-visit destination. Windsor Castle has been standing for centuries, and its Changing of the Guard ceremony is sure to leave you in awe. Windsor Horse Show, held in Windsor Great Park every spring, is another great attraction worth visiting – offering thrilling equestrian displays, spectacular shows and competitions, as well as stalls full of traditional and modern goods. The Long Walk is 2 miles long and provides magnificent views of Windsor Castle, Windsor Great Park, the River Thames and its surrounding countryside. Its wide pavement is perfect for a leisurely stroll, making it an ideal spot for taking memorable photos! Whether you are looking for a peaceful getaway or want to explore Windsor's beautiful scenery and vibrant atmosphere, The Long Walk is the perfect choice. With its green open spaces, picturesque views and easy accessibility, Windsor's Long Walk is the ideal spot to make lasting memories.

And don't forget to take a look at Henry VIII's gate Windsor castle and glimpse Cromwell's procuration on wall. Be mesmerized by the fountains by Windsor Maze and enjoy the beauty of Windsor Great Park! Have a great visit to Windsor!

Printed in Great Britain
by Amazon

20057670R00016